A GORDONS GALLIMAUFRY

A Gordons Gallimaufry

collected by
Major Leslie Hatt, TD

illustrated by
Jane Habgood

All proceeds to Lt-Gen. Sir Peter Graham's Museum Campaign
for The Gordon Highlanders Museum at the Regimental HQ,
Viewfield Road, Aberdeen.

PARAPRESS LTD
Tunbridge Wells · Kent

Acknowledgements

I should like to thank John Bennett for the free use of the cover
illustration, Major Pat Ellis for thinking up the title,
Sir Peter Graham for his encouragement, my grandson
Ian Parker for his work as a 'go for', and everyone who contributed
a portion to the 'gallimaufry'.

First published in the UK in 1995 by
PARAPRESS LTD
12 Dene Way
Speldhurst
Tunbridge Wells
Kent TN3 0NX

© Leslie Hatt 1995

ISBN 1-898594-65-1

British Library Cataloguing in Publication Data:
A catalogue record for this book is available from the British Library

Typeset by Vitaset, Paddock Wood, Kent.

Printed in Great Britain by
Biddles Ltd, Guildford and King's Lynn.

Contents

1. The Second Man Wins

I was with the Gordons, in the 2nd Armoured Brigade of the 1st Armoured Division. It was almost at the end of the Alamein battle in early November 1942; after breaking through the first of the enemy's lines, we had just finished 'topping up' our tanks with ammunition. We had the enemy's wire behind us, and there were still a number of them causing trouble.

'Ginger' Creese and I were standing by our Canadian Chev' 3-tonner when the 'opposition' must have called down an artillery stonk. For the tanks this didn't pose much of a problem, but for a 'soft' vehicle like ours the only thing was to go to ground very quickly.

A rapid glance showed us a slit trench about sixty yards away, so both Ginger and I were away like greyhounds (I had done quite a bit of running, and he was a good rugby player). This time I was ahead with about six yards to go for the trench when I felt a hand grab my shirt and Ginger leapt past me and dived in, with me flopping on top of him into it.

'It' turned out to be the correct word, because the enemy ex-occupants had used one end as a latrine. The smell was terrible, but unlike Ginger I didn't have to get rid of my khaki drill shirt and shorts. You can guess the state of his. Believe me I was lucky, and grateful, to have come second on that occasion!

P.A.R. Bartlett

2. Inspection Cover

During the 1st Battalion's tour in Berlin in 1949-50, the weekly inspection of Company lines took place every Saturday morning. The Commanding Officer, Lt-Col. V.D.G. Campbell, inspected three of the six barrack blocks at Montgomery Barracks and the 2nd In Command, Major Ross (Conger), inspected the remaining three one week; and the following week the CO and 2nd I/C exchanged their inspection areas.

I was Company Sergeant Major of Specialist Company, and on muster parade on a certain Saturday morning I spoke to all the Platoon Sergeants and informed them that our inspecting officer would be the CO. The Sp. Coy. NAAFI break was scheduled for 1000 -1030 hours and, this being the case, no-one was to be allowed into the barrack block during the inspection.

At about 0950 hours the Officer Commanding Specialist Company called on me to accompany him to the door to meet the inspecting team. On passing the entrance to the toilet and urinal section, I heard someone move, and on further investigation I found Private Craig in one of the cubicles, fully dressed. When I questioned him he made no excuse. I shut the door and told him to stay there until the inspection was past.

The urinal trough being blocked, the CO remarked to the Quarter Master, Major MacDonald, that the place smelled a bit high. The Major said that the barrack engineers had been notified and were working on it.

The CO was a stickler for the proper Army form-blank being in the box provided behind the toilet doors, and proceeded to push these open with his cane. I wondered how Craig would react when he was confronted, but I didn't have long to wait for the answer. The third cubicle door the

CO opened was pushed close from the inside. This happened three times, and when the CO eventually opened it there was Craig sitting on the pot fully dressed.

'And what are you doing?' asked the CO.

'The Sergeant told me to stay here until after the inspection, Sir.'

The inspection team had a good laugh.

Jock Rainine

3. Fighting in the Gothic Line, Italy 1944

I was instructed to report to the Battalion HQ, which was on another ridge about two miles away. Brown, my faithful batman, and I set off – the day was very hot and we had to cross the valley and climb up to the other ridge. After I had received my orders we made our way back to the Company HQ.

In the valley there was a small stream and, having perspired in the heat, I decided to have a 'dook' in the 'wee burn'. Quickly divesting ourselves of our clothes, we found a small pool and sat down in the cool water. We were enjoying the refreshing dip, when all of a sudden there was a 'whoosh' and loud bang, as a shell exploded about 100 yards to our right. Thought: Must be an overshot from somewhere. Then a few minutes later another shell exploded about 50 yards to our left, showering us with stones and dirt.

Brown said quite calmly, 'I think we should shift, Sir, before the next one comes.' We did just that: boots and shorts on and we took off through the cordite fumes. But no more shells came our way.

"Och come back you've forgotten your shoe!"

4. A Night Exercise on the Links Course at Aberdeen During the War

We had to proceed in pairs at ten minute intervals and try and penetrate the enemy positions at the other end of the course. We had gone some distance, when a sudden noise made us dive into a small bunker. Unfortunately, we landed on top of a couple evidently in a very close embrace. Amid cries of surprise all round, they managed to disentangle themselves. The couple got to their feet and fled in the direction of our enemy. We followed hard behind them in the hope that the positions would be revealed to us.

There was a cry of 'halt', and some shouting and scuffling, enabling us to slip through the enemy posts during the commotion. I recall, at the debriefing, the enemy officer's report:

'We apprehended two figures in the dark – a man and a woman – both were in a dishevelled state, the woman having lost a shoe. Both were incoherent and shocked. I placed them in custody, as I thought they were "fifth columnists". They were released at the end of the exercise. The enemy, with torches, eventually recovered the lady's shoe in the bunker.'

(We did not mention the incident in the bunker, as we were the only pair to infiltrate the enemy defences that evening.)

Major MacHardy

"I don't know what he's saying Sarge I don't speak Scottish!".

5. It's All in the Meaning

One of the tasks I was employed on as a prisoner of war of the Japanese was the construction of a shrine on a hill behind the Ford Factory at Bukit Timah. One day as we left the site we passed an Australian group who were also preparing to finish: 'Hey, Scotties, listen to this; we have taught this little bastard how to say "Dismiss" in good Aussie.'

As he spoke, a Japanese soldier trudged forward and climbed up on a heap of earth topped with a surveyor's marker. He acknowledged the calls of encouragement he received (obviously he assumed they were calls of encouragement, or otherwise he would have made a few placatory prayers to his ancestors), took in a large breath, then shouted out at the top of his voice, 'All men piss off!'

With a huge grin he acknowledged the cheers he received, convinced he had got the accent just right!

6. A Sticky Encounter

I had reached my sixteenth birthday less than three weeks previously and was now aboard HMS *Ettrick* on my way to join my regiment, 2nd Battalion Gordon Highlanders, in Singapore.

I was high with excited impatience: HMS *Ettrick* was approaching the Grand Harbour at Valletta. I desperately wanted to be up on deck to view this place I had heard so much about, but first I had to finish my duty as dining table orderly. I hurried away from the galley with an oval shaped

The Gordon Highlanders definition of debriefing!

two-gallon dixie, containing hot tapioca pudding.

Disaster struck when I slipped on the top step of the open gangway. As I crashed to the bottom, still clutching the handle of the now empty dixie, the contents disappeared between the open steps, and it was from under these steps that I heard bellows of rage, interspersed with the most fearsome, life-threatening oaths.

The sight under the companion-way filled me with horror. A very large sailor had just completed dressing himself to go ashore, but now streaks of tapioca pudding were coursing down his immaculate white shirt and carefully pressed trousers from large deposits of the stuff on his cap and shoulders. His face was brick red and his hands clenched into two massive fists.

I could not move, and gazed in panic as he spat out at me through tightly closed teeth, 'Just don't say sorry!'

I didn't. I scurried away down to the mess-deck, ready with my excuse for no pudding. I need not have bothered: everyone was up on deck watching the ship enter harbour.

Archie Black

7. Fish Lorry South

After five gruelling weeks of basic training, we were given our first week-end leave, from Friday to Sunday. I decided to head home to Glasgow, and offered to take Peter Badger, who came from Sheffield, with me. Not wishing to be left on his own in the barrack room, he jumped at the offer.

To save money, we decided to hitch-hike, and our first lift took us to Stonehaven, where we had been told the fish

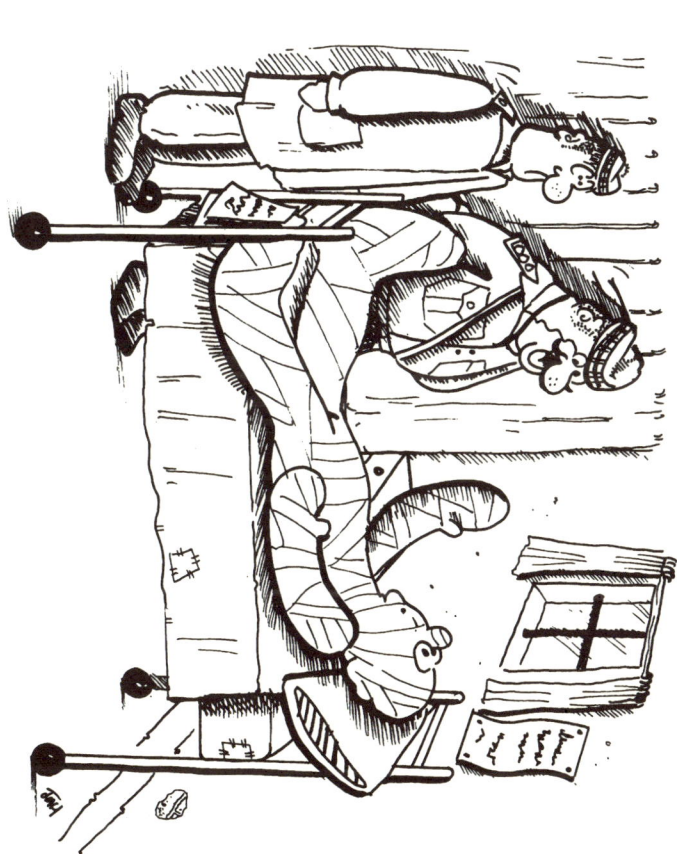

"And so tell me young chap, where were you wounded?"

lorries heading south started coming through about 7pm. Because we were hungry and had some time to spare, we went into a café in the main street for a cup of tea and bacon rolls. While there, we got speaking to a few of the locals, who asked how we were enjoying Army life.

'Not very much,' I replied, or words to that effect. I believe I may have also made a few uncomplimentary remarks about our platoon NCOs.

Eventually we arrived at my parents' house at about 3am, and a great fuss was made of us: you would have thought we had been away for years, instead of five weeks. We had a great week-end.

Pete and I travelled back to Aberdeen on Sunday, by train. We checked into the guardroom in good time and then prepared our kit for the next day.

On parade on Monday morning, our Platoon Sergeant screamed:

'Badger, McKenzie, one place forward, march! The next time you two idiots are in a café in Stonehaven, don't tell my brother I am a torn-faced old bastard!'

I still laugh about that incident to this day.

Bill McKenzie

8. The Swindle of the Roast Chicken

At Mahon Paton sick camp, a British Other Ranks came into the cookhouse and said, 'Anybody want to buy a chicken?' He wanted two dollars, which was worth very little in Thailand under the Japs. So the cook gave him the price, and he then left in a hurry.

18

"Er jimmy da ya think that goats get jealous ?"

When the cookhouse lads opened its wrapper, they saw that the bird had rather thick legs. 'It's not a chicken,' said one, 'it's a "vulter".' Then the Dutch interpreter for the Japs came in, so the cook said, 'Do you want to buy a chicken? We will roast it for you.' So the interpreter, his mouth watering, said 'That's grand, it will do for Headquarters' Mess.'

The bird was duly eaten that night. Some of the officers found it disagreed with them and were sick, and some had sore tummies next day; so a few days afterwards they were told the real story.

William Merchant

9. No soft option

The troops wanted to know why they were not getting soft boiled eggs for breakfast. I decided that they should have them, but when I told the duty cook to give them soft boiled eggs, he replied that he had boiled them for half an hour, but they were still hard.

C. Shand

10. The Bachle Clerk

The Battalion had just completed one year's tour of Borneo and had a well earned six weeks' leave, and was now re-forming back in Redford Barracks. Kit checks and tailor

'What Message?'

"Well Private McKay - if your name
is on it'..... that's it."

parades were the order of the day, plus constant company drill parades to get ready for public duties. Ceremonial kit was to be issued to every man, from the CO to the youngest Jock.

In the summer of '66 the Battalion Annual Inspection was coming up, and it would take the form of a ceremonial parade. The preparations for this were vast: whiten spats, press kilt, fit jacket, refit jacket, Brasso belt buckle. Then came the day of inspection. The Battalion formed up on Cavalry Barracks Square, with Drums and Pipes and Military Band to the rear of the parade.

The inspecting Brigadier arrives and the inspection begins, and of course it seems to take forever. At last he comes round to the Drums and Pipes. Drummie Hall pays the Brigy the normal compliments and informs him, 'Drums and Pipes ready for your inspection, Sir!'

Walking along the ranks, checking here, asking questions there, the Brigadier confronts Piper Hobby, 'The Bachle Clerk'.

'And who are you?' he asks.

'Och,' says Hobby, quite confident in himself, 'Nae bad; foo's yersel, sir?'

Everyone within earshot, CO, Company Commander, Drum Major, Pipe Major, their faces were a picture. Sheer discipline prevented them from bursting out with laughter. I don't know if the Brigadier realised that he had greeted Hobby in typical North East fashion, but by the time he was finished, Hobby had given him his service record, marital status, state of quarters, and how his two children were getting on at school.

Result of Inspection Report: 'Excellent'.

Ian Whyte

11. My Friend's Father's Favourite Story:
Private Alex Barclay MM, Gordon Highlanders
1914-18.

It seems that the morning 'hate' was in full swing on Alex's sector of the Western Front, and assorted pieces of iron whined, buzzed, roared and banged through the air of *la belle France*. Artillery and mortars spread various pieces of Krupp steel over the landscape, together with large pieces of the said landscape.

Suddenly . . . silence, except for a few stones and lumps of mud falling back to earth! A mud-spattered helmet stirred itself and was cautiously raised . . . a wondering voice in broadest Buchan rang through the dust, smoke and cordite fumes . . . 'Siccan a steer, siccan a steer!'

Alex has gone to his last parade now, but I always thought it was a disappointment to him when his son served in the next brawl in the Royal Navy, and I ended up in the Sappers.

James Watt

12. A True Tale about 14049605 Private Wilson, now 68 years young but with a clear memory of over fifty years ago.

I was eighteen years old, and had completed my six weeks' initial training at Pinefield Camp, near Elgin. My posting was to the Gordon Highlanders at Bridge of Don Barracks, Aberdeen, for further training before being posted overseas and on active service.

"Of course its porridge son, what did you expect from the Gordon Highlanders - tea + crumpets?"

I had been detailed for guard duty at the entrance to Gordon Barracks. It was three in the morning, and a nasty night weather-wise, drizzle with fog. As I sheltered in the sentry box, asleep on my feet, a voice suddenly shouted in my ear:

'Have you a licence for that gun?'

Whereupon I dropped my .303 on the ground with a clatter. Into the shadows disappeared an Aberdeen Bobbie, complete with dark cloak. Whilst I retrieved my Lee Enfield, he went on his way roaring with laughter.

George S. Wilson

13. A Matter of Urgency

It was 1938 and the Territorial Army had had to be doubled. On one occasion, two hundred recruits were on parade. Sergeant-majors with pace sticks were rushing around shouting, 'Be still in the ranks!' The tallest men were on the flanks and the shortest in the middle.

Suddenly there was pandemonium. The shortest chap in the front had laid his rifle on the ground and marched off the parade ground.

That night the CO said, 'Charles, why did you march off parade?'

Charles was the Marquis of Huntly; he considered that nobody was going to decide when he could or couldn't go to the toilet:

'I wanted a shit, and went and had a shit.'

Anon

"Och Sir there's a fella here says he'll gee us five Camels and two goats for the wee lass in the skirt see the nice legs!"

14. Stranger Than Fiction

In 1939 the War Council decided to send a fighting force
to Orkney, in case Hitler decided to do a right-flanker and
invade the UK.

So, a month before war broke out, 100 Gordon
Highlanders met their leader, a 2nd Lieutenant, at Aberdeen
Harbour before embarking for Orkney. Each man was
wearing Field Service Marching Order, plus 50 rounds, but
G1098 stores consisted of a bren gun and a latrine bucket
and cover.

Before boarding our vessel, the Quarter Sergeant
approached me saying, 'We have no rations, Sir.'

Decision time! Was it to be the Princess Café, with
mutton pie and chips for everyone, or was it to be Lumsden
and Gibson, for the provision of oatmeal, sugar, tea, sausage,
bacon etc.?

I decided on Lumsden and Gibson, and the flummoxed
manager was left looking at a bill signed by myself, in the
name of King George VI.

When the vessel arrived at Kirkwall harbour, we were
met by our new master: a captain of the Lovat Scouts. 'There
is a problem,' he said. 'No transport.' 'Don't worry,' I said.
An hour later, the local undertaker had lost his runaround,
a Daimler, and the local school had lost its twenty-seater
bus. The formula of requisitioning in the name of King
George VI had prevailed, and we were in business.

One NCO and Section were despatched to the island
of Hoy. The weather was very bad in that part of the world,
and we never met again. Our leader started to get anxious
about the Section, so he arranged for a drifter to take him
there. Weeks passed, and there was no word of the Section,
our leader, or the latrine bucket, so senior 2nd Lieutenant
Hatt became OC home forces of Orkney, and had to liaise

"Jack forget about that
look at the size of
the one i've just found"

with the Admiral of the Fleet, Sir Charles Forbes.

The fleet was in Scapa Flow, and a trawler took me to the flagship. Sir Charles was in a beautiful walnut-lined cabin. The interview was not a success, as he did not want to hear about the latrine bucket going to Hoy, nor about the Bren gun defending the airfield at Netherbottom.

The headquarters of our force was stationed at the schoolhouse at Holm, which was at the entrance of Scapa. A chain had been left there, spanning the entrance, since 1918. One night a Submarine Fuhrer took his craft over the boom. Reaching his base at Kiel, he remarked that he thought he had been spotted by a searchlight. This was our school bus going about its duties, and the headlights had caused consternation on the sub.

As this had happened at one o' clock in the morning, it was supposed that there had been a romantic episode, and fault was laid at the feet of the 2nd Lieutenant. To say that his departure from Orkney was under a cloud, would be an understatement.

Major Leslie Hatt, TD

15. Near Roubaix, May 1940

The late Dr J. Lennel Taylor, the RMO, had established his Regimental Aid Post in the small town of Hem, and he told his staff: 'We're a' richt, lads, we're Hem noo.'

Orders were given to put all surplus equipment out of action, to prevent it falling into German hands, and one Banffie, toiling with a Boyes Anti-tank gun, promptly threw away the bolt, but kept on carrying the heavy gun.

I don't care if your granny did knit them O'Brien
You're not wearing them in this regiment !!!

16. Hammamet

Sweltering under the hot Tunisian sun on the second Tuesday in August 1943, one Keith loon remarked to another: 'Weel, th're gettin' a gran' day for the Keith Show.'

17. Anzio, February 1944

B Echelon was being heavily shelled and attacked from the air with Anti-Personnel and High Explosive bombs, and all the men were keeping their heads down in the slit trenches and dug-outs, except one. A senior NCO, with 'a good shot in', was walking about in the open with all the 'shit' falling around, shaking his fists and shouting to the sky, 'Awa to your bloody beds!' Later on that night, a 'dud' shell passed under his dugout, causing it to collapse. When we dug him out he was still smiling and still bleezing, with not a mark on him.

Keith Boardman
(No. 2881639 – I still remember it!)

18. Vino Por Soldati

In August 1944, when B Echelon moved into Florence, I was developing jaundice. When the MO noticed my saffron complexion, I ended up in a general hospital in Naples. In

Sir, the Butts Have Said - 'Now we've Pasted up the warden, is there any chance of you aiming at the Target Please!?...

this hospital, standing orders stated that Bed Patients must lie to attention, but Up Patients could sit to attention.

After discharge, I renewed an acquaintance with a man whose father had extensive vineyards at Radda in Chianti, who offered considerable discounts. I informed the President of Regimental Institutes, who told me to get on with it as Christmas was getting near.

The expedition set off in the snow: a 15cwt truck, driver, servant, Transport Officer, wine taster and interpreter, me, 2 carboys, 2 days' rations and cigarettes for barter if necessary. In the main street I asked for Il Commandante (I had been tipped off with use of rank). A number of army personnel saluted, men removed hats and caps, elderly women curtsied and a satisfactory number of young ladies rolled their eyes and other parts of their anatomies at my soldiers. I considered that Man Management was completed.

I then met my host (saluting, etc. redoubled). Telling Il Commandante that I would like to get the truck under cover for the night, I received the surprising suggestion that it would be quite safe in the kitchen. When I went in through the double doors, I realised that the kitchen would probably have held two 15cwts and a jeep.

Next I was escorted to the Big House and introduced to the family, which mainly consisted of elderly spinsters. Most of the conversation was carried on in rough French, but a variety of chianti, up to a vintage brew of 25 years old, is a great leveller.

I don't remember the food.

At a late hour (never trust an elderly Italian spinster when you are being entertained by a chianti producer) I was told that my bed was ready and that it would be nice and warm as The Priest was in it and had been there for two hours. Now, I am reasonably broad-minded about religion,

"What's the point of my staying on in the Army if we're going to row every time I'm late in the morning"

but I did feel that this was carrying things a bit too far. They fell about laughing and eventually explained that The Priest was a construction, rather like a sleigh in shape, made of cane with curved side pieces and a charcoal pot suspended in the middle. The charcoal is alight, and, when you get into the bed, the whole outfit is put underneath it to warm the room.

This joke lasted us through breakfast, and delayed it considerably, so when we had loaded up our two big carboys, we set off through the snow, which was hiding the potholes and bumps, and put on a bit of a spurt. We hit a bump bigger that usual and there was a yell from the rear. We pulled up and got out. The language from the back was really blue. A bung had come out, and my servant had received about seven gallons of first class vino all over his clothing.

By the time we got back, the smell had disappeared from his greatcoat, but I was subsequently informed that it would fluctuate with the temperature, and when it thawed out it became impossible to wear inside.

Personally, I blame The Priest.

Major Curran Douglas, TD

19. The Doctor and the Ambulance

My Battalion was on a long tour in Palace Barracks, Belfast. I had a Regimental Medical Officer who loved to go round the Barracks in his little Landrover ambulance with the blue light flashing and siren sounding! Every time I heard the sound, I thought somebody was injured, so he was told to stop it.

"You're an 'Orrible little man!
What are you?"

Late one Saturday night a Jock fell down the stairs. He dislocated his shoulder and reported to the Medical Centre. The doctor was called for and decided the injury was sufficient to warrant him taking the young man into the Musgrave Park Hospital. He called for the Landrover ambulance and the soldier was put on a stretcher in the back; the doctor got into the front and off they sped into Belfast, to the doctor's delight with siren sounding and blue lights flashing!

They jumped a set of traffic lights, and as a result had a head-on collision with a car. With the shock of the accident, the rear doors of the ambulance flew open: out flew the Jock on his stretcher, hit the ground, and the shoulder went back into place! Meanwhile the doctor shot through the windscreen, and twenty minutes later he was in hospital while the Jock was safe and sound in his barrack room!

20. My Six Points

When I commanded the Ulster Defence Regiment, I decided from the outset that there was a need to concentrate the soldiers' minds on certain aspects of their training. Pride, alertness, discipline, fitness, shooting and co-operation became a byword throughout the Regiment. Before starting a conversation, I would often stop and ask soldiers what the 'six points' were. Certain commanding officers produced stickers with them printed on so that people would remember them.

Late one evening I was with the Commanding Officer

"And who may I ask, gave Pte. Flinn permission to grow a 'Pony Tail'?"

of the 3rd Battalion, The Ulster Defence Regiment and we were visiting some of his patrols. It was quite a light night. We came across a patrol which was very near a skyline: one could see the outline of figures in the patrol, as they lay on a bank. In the distance you could see one figure who, every now and again, appeared to take off his beret and scratch his head. He kept on doing it. We got near, and I said to him, 'Is there something wrong with your head? Have you got fleas or something?'

In a broad Ulster accent he informed me, 'I knew it was you, I saw you coming and I am trying to remember your six points, which are on a sticker in the inside of my beret, but I can't read the bastards.'

21. Nicknames

During my time in command of the 1st Battalion The Gordon Highlanders in Northern Ireland, one of our young officers, whilst on patrol, was involved in an ambush incident. After it was all over, he forgot to unload his weapon and accidentally put a shot into his foot. Fortunately for him it only nicked one of his toes. Thereafter he was always known as NATO (Nae Toe) Pearson.

The Colonel of my Regiment, Lieutenant General Sir George Gordon Lennox, a great warrior, decided that he would visit the 1st Battalion in Belfast. During lunch I recounted the story of 'NATO' Pearson. The old boy was not going to be outdone; he had been a Grenadier in his early days. He turned to me and said, 'Well, Peter, in my other Regiment we had a chap who accidentally shot his father, and thereafter he was always known as "Baghdad"!'

"Apparently it was the last bottle of Glenfiddich"

22. Medical Anecdotes

When I commanded the 1st Battalion the Gordon Highlanders, we left Northern Ireland and took over Saighton Camp, near Chester. We were then made the Spearhead Battalion for the United Kingdom, which meant we had to be prepared to fly out at very short notice to any trouble spot. This required a great deal of preparation, not least of which was the medical preparations.

The Medical Sergeant in the Battalion was, curiously enough, a Welshman, Sergeant Hamilton. He was a great character, and on one of the many conferences designed to check that we were progressing in our preparations, he complained bitterly that it was extremely difficult to get the Battalion together so that they all received the necessary injections.

'Sir', he said, 'If you give me the whole Battalion for one afternoon, I will kill it.'

On another occasion I got rather irritated because there were still a number of injections outstanding. I felt he could put a little more energy into completing this and I said to him, 'There are twenty-six polio injections outstanding, Sergeant Hamilton. Indeed I am one of them, and it would not be funny if I went stiff with polio this afternoon!'

'Sir!' was Hamilton's reply, 'If you went stiff this afternoon, all my worries would be over!'

Lt-Gen. Sir Peter Graham, KCB CBE

"Och no no nurse, I said remove the patients Spectacles"

23. A Highland Happening

One of the Gordon Highlanders' happenings which sticks in my mind was the occasion when Prince Charles visited the 1st Battalion as Colonel-in-Chief. The visit was near the end of a hard exercise, when the companies were harbouring in some woods, just before being flown into a final action by helicopter. Weapons had been cleaned, ammunition replenished and orders given out, and the Colonel-in-Chief went round talking to as many of the Jocks as he could. At the final company position, the Company Commander took him to where one of the platoons was supposed to be, and found just one private soldier, lying on his back with his mouth wide open, snoring like a train. His mates had sneaked quietly away about twenty yards, knowing that he alone would represent them on the royal walkabout.

Despite the Prince's tactful whispering in the presence of the epitome of the Highland soldier, a fly flew so close to the open mouth that the snore was interrupted, the soldier eased one eye open, and beheld the heir to the throne peering intently at him from two or three feet away. The expressions that crossed his face as consciousness returned were puzzlement, disbelief, a terrible feeling that something catastrophic had happened, and at last a dawning.

As he tried to get his legs to heave him into a more respectful position, the other thought that clearly flashed through his mind was, 'I'll get the bastards for dropping me in it like this!'

Lt-Gen. Sir John Macmillan, KCB CBE

24. A Rehearsal

Back in 1972 the Military Band of the Gordons was serving in Singapore. Once every five years the Band had to be inspected by the Director of Kneller Hall. The inspection covered everything: music, accounts, stores, library, and the one every bandsman loves best: drill and bearing on parade.

The Bandmaster thought it would help if the Regimental Sergeant Major took us for some drill. Each minstrel was wearing at least fifty pieces of equipment from spats to feather bonnet, and in this we had to play and slow march at the same time.

The RSM walked backwards in front of us, screaming 'Downwards and outwards! Downwards and outwards!', the drill for the slow march.

Then calamity struck downwards and outwards, as the RSM fell backwards over a hedge. He was still shouting 'Downwards and outwards,' as we slow-marched past his two feet sticking in the air, but he lacked the same resolution.

Meanwhile, the 2nd In Command, who was Band President, said,'Oh, look, Bandmaster, the RSM has fallen over.'

A. Reid Esq.

25. Apocrypha

Twa auld Gordons in the Grill Bar meeting up for the first time in years:

Wullie says tae Jimmy, 'Fit like a wife hiv ye got?' Jimmy replies 'She's just an angel.' Wullie says, 'Och! you're lucky; mines is aye living!'

Lt-Col. R.D. Strachan, MBE

When the 9th Gordons first encountered approaching Japanese Kamikaze troops, an excited Jock yelled to his Company Commander, 'The hale lot are goin' tae commit Kama Sutra!'

A wounded Jock of the 9th Gordons was visited in hospital by General Slim, who asked him where he had been wounded. 'Weel, Sir,' replied Willie, 'It would be about twa-three miles on the Huntly side o' the Irrawaddy.'

Two Jocks were sitting cleaning their weapons when General Alexander came along, but as they did not recognise him they did not bother to get up. Looking down, he growled, 'Do you know who I am?'

One of the Jocks yelled over to the medical orderly. 'Hey, Smith, there's a poor bloke here fa' disna ken his name!'

Some Bedford people in 1914 were amused when one raw Banffshire Jock who had never seen a vegetable marrow asked the stall-holder, 'Foo muckle for the big banana?'

Lt-Col. Donald Young, TD BA FBIM

48

26. Fa' Shot the Cheese?

Major George Thom, late of the Gordons, told me this story:

The incident took place on the Somme in November 1916, when the 6th Gordons were in reserve.

At the main ration dump at Crucifix Corner, there was a railway embankment with a concealed sunken road at the bottom. On top of the embankment the Royal Engineers had laid a track. One night, on this track, the ration party of an English regiment was making its way up to its reserve position, with all their rations loaded on one handcart. These included a massive round cheese.

Meanwhile the ration party of the 7th Gordons was moving with their rations up the sunken road, practically abreast of the English party.

The cheese, however, fell off the cart and rolled down the hill towards the Gordons, accompanied by a shindy of yells and curses from the English. What ensued was related by a sergeant of the 6th Gordons who, with true Banff-Donside modesty, not wishing to give all the honour of winning the war to the 6th Gordons, gives credit to the 7th for their glorious action:

> An Epic of the Somme, 1916
> or
> 'Fa' Shot the Cheese?'
>
> We didn't go in for flashy stunts,
>   We merely played our part
> But were as hard a lot to stop
>   As any that did start;
> But oh, the seventh from Deeside
>   Earned fame o'er all the seas
> By their famous stand on that awful night
>   When they killed the charging cheese.

A noble hand the rations bore
    Up from the peaceful rear,
Alert each man to his duty grim
    And strangers all to fear,
And little recked of the part they'd play
    Or how hard would go the fight
When they alone would stem the foe
    On that now historic night.

They marched along, a silent band,
    By the side of a lonely hill,
When sudden the evening's quiet was rent
    By a sound both loud and shrill.
Each heart beat high in its manly breast,
    For each scarred warrior knew
That sound could only mean one thing:
    The Bosche had broken through.

Halted the band, and the Quarty spoke:
    'Ye lads whom I now command
Have a part to play, a noble part,
    For the sake of the Motherland.'
Then he turned his face to the charging foe
    And he yelled o'er the evening air;
Like a clarion blast his voice pealed forth:
    'Halt! Halt! Halt, who goes there?'

The foe rushed on, while the Quarty grim
    To his shoulder raised his gun.
He swore aloud that he alone
    Must kill the leading Hun.
The rifle spoke, the bullet flew,
    Its course was quickly sped,
And in half the time it takes to tell
    The charging foe lay dead.

"Oh dear, I think you've hit the bull!"

The ration party shouldered hipes
 And went to find their prey.
They wanted to share the foeman's goods,
 For such is our Quarty's way.
But joy within their hearts was quelled
 And curses rent the breeze,
When Quarty found to his dire dismay
 That he's shot a bloody cheese.

Now this is a tale of long ago
 Which is remembered still
By the sweats of Banff and Donside
 Who the old Sixth ranks did fill;
And if e'er you want to start a row
 And crave mercy from your knees,
Just say to a man from the stalwart Seventh,
 'Hey, Jock, fa' shot the cheese?'

The original was signed W.S.D., Courcelette-Ovillers, October 1916.   **Dr L. Mackie**

27. The Hero

He was a gallant Highlander,
 A bold and fearless man,
All alone and single-handed
 He killed them, every one.

He was up against a thousand,
 Or maybe even more:
And he laid them all around him
 Like pebbles on the shore.

He received no decoration,
    He got no word of praise,
Yet he felt more free and easy
    Than he had done for days.

He asked no ammunition
    No help from bursting shells;
He killed each louse upon his shirt
    By using his finger nails.

These verses were written by my late father, Albert Mc-
Andrew, who was in the Gordon Highlanders during the First
World War. They were actually written on scraps of paper
while he was in the trenches in France.

Mrs Isma Munro

28. The Man Who Gave His All

As 7015063 Private J.A. Whelan, serving in D Company 6th
Gordons in Tunisia, I was advancing through the sparse
wheat to attack Point 212, when I had an argument with a
belligerent object known as an anti-personnel mine, which
endeavoured to make a culinary utensil of my testis.

After a few weeks in a field hospital, I beat the 'Y' listing
system, and returned to 6th Gordons.

Tunis had then fallen to the Allies, and parades etc.
were the order of the day, with training for further
conquests. I was given my first stripe and was put on a cadre
course for NCOs.

On the first morning we paraded for the CO's

inspection. Lt-Col Peddie came along the ranks. He stopped in front of me, looked me straight in the eye, and in his dry, witty way he said to me, 'Ah, Whelan, the man who gave his b . . . . . all for his country.'

J.A. Whelan

29. Div y' Min'?

Div y' min' on cocky Hunter's,
'n' his junk at Castle Hill?
Div y' min' on Soapy Ogston's
Reid & Pearson's, Watt & Milne?

Div y' min' on cha'k and inkwells,
Slate and pincils at th' school?
Div y' min' on Co-op Divi's,
'n' checks – tied up wi' wool?

Div y' min' on Bookies' Runners;
Crown & Anchor at the Links?
Black-leaded grates and ovens;
Brass taps in cast-iron sinks?

Div y' min' on wash-hoose bilers,
And Mangles sair tae ca'?
And squares o' paper hung wi' string
On a reed-ochered lavvy wa'?

The watch and chain that grand-da wore
'n' granny's crooshied shawl?
Div y' really min' on a' these things?
By God . . . yer gettin' aul!!

Mr A. Findlay

54

30. A Pearl of Wisdom

This pearl was cast at us while we were National Service Officer Cadets at Eaton Hall in 1952 by RSM Copp of the Guards on his Monday morning parades, when we young cadets were still recovering from the excesses of the week-end:

'I'll call you "Sir", and you'll call me "Sir" – but remember this, Sir, only one of us bloody well means it!'

Mike Robson

31. More Apocrypha

A sergeant in the Gordon Highlanders drilling his men near the pyramids found that their eyes kept wandering towards the monuments.

'What are ye glowering at?' he bellowed. 'A great rickle o' auld stanes! Hae ye no seen Bennachie?'

Ian G. McIntosh

During the '14-18 War, the Gordon Highlanders and the Highland Light Infantry were involved under General Allenby in Palestine. In a hostelry one night, an argument arose between a Gordon and a Highland Light Infantry private as to which regiment first entered Bethlehem to liberate it from the Turks.

After a heated discussion it became clear that the Gordon had lost the argument. 'Aw Weel,' says he, 'If ye were in afore us, I bet the shepherds watched their flocks that night.'

Tom D. Robertson, FOTGH

I was on duty as Orderly Corporal in the dining room at Badajoz Barracks, Aldershot, in 1939. At lunch time a young English officer asked if there were any complaints about the meal. Up spoke one of the lads in broad Aberdeen Doric: 'The tatties are hard, Sir.'

'What does he mean, Sergeant?' said the officer.

'Oh, the man's ingerent, Sir, he means the spuds.' The officer shook his head, as if wondering what the hell sort of foreigners he had been drafted to.

Bydand for Ever

Jock Stewart, No. 2877831.

32. Hogmanay

It was New Year's Eve 1944-5 and the Battalion was on the river Maas, with companies spread out along the river. HQ was in a large chateau just a short distance behind. As was normal under these conditions, hot food was sent forward after dark to the platoons on or near the river bank.

This however was rather a special night: Hogmanay! I don't know how they managed it, but every Jock had somehow kept a tot or two of whisky to celebrate. Not knowing what I was in for, I set off after midnight with my batman, to visit all the company positions.

At every post and slit trench it was the same: 'A dram for the New Year, Sir!' Who could refuse? Who would wish to refuse?

By the time I was nearing my company HQ on completion, I realised that I was incapable of coherent thought or action, and had enough sense to lie down in a chicken hut for a couple of hours to sober up. After a while, and feeling quite terrible, I entered Company HQ, to receive a message to report to Battalion HQ forthwith.

I imagined that I had been wanted during the night, had not been available, and in consequence was about to receive my marching orders. Slowly making my way to the magnificent chateau, I met other company commanders who if anything were in a worse state than me. It was then obvious that this was normal in a Highland Regiment. The order to attend was to receive a situation report from the CO.

It was a blessing the enemy did not choose to mount a counter attack – it would have been hard going!

Major Leslie Grose, MC

33. Short on Memory

The Battalion was stationed at the frontier of Afghanistan. My Platoon Sergeant was a Highlander from the North of Scotland. One day, while supervising the issue of rations to the companies, he told the orderly piper who was on duty to play 'Rations'.

But the piper had forgotten the tune.

Sergeant Simpson, who was a large man, over six feet tall, told us that 'He whistled the tune, he sang the tune, and he even danced the tune, but the piper could not make contact.'

George Morrice, MM

"Aaaagh you've caught my tie"

34. Aquatic

An Indian dhobi was dislodged from his washing stone by a passing boat, and was the recipient of the following Buchan-cum-Indian advice from an observing Jock:

'If TUM had JILDIED when I BOLOED ye widna have fallen in the bloody PANI.'

Major F.J.R. Moir

35. The Potter's Tale

'Son, the whole wide world is in front of you, and half the Australian Police Force is behind you.'

So, on a Sydney Harbour dock, circa 1938, young Charles Stewart, later to be known to a generation of Gordon Highlanders as Aussie, Potter, was propelled to Europe and World War II.

On a cold spring morning in 1960, in Celle, West Germany, all of the Gordons' Provost Staff were behind him.

Private Potter, in his accustomed state of inebriated semi-consciousness, and attired as usual in battledress (he didn't possess civvies), three rows of decorations with oak leaf, and Tam o' Shanter worn à la Digger, was augmenting his supply of Deutsch marks.

Aussie had a prodigious thirst for Myers' rum, and his schemes to procure this commodity were legendary. On this occasion he had liberated a quantity of prime beef from the cookhouse and was hawking it around the married quarters. Eventually captured, he was put in Bert Buchan's 'Hotel' to await Colonel George Elsmie's disposal the following morn.

I'd just taken down my pipes after reveille when all hell broke loose in the guardroom. A National Service provost corporal from Banchory was trying to wake Aussie, and Aussie, who as a rule drank two Coca-cola bottles of neat rum before attempting anything so foolhardy, wasn't having it.

The situation was solved by the hotel's wily proprietor, Provost Sergeant Albert Buchan, who brought from the Sergeants' Mess a liberal measure of old vatted Demerara. Eventually, in a borrowed kilt and my best boots, Aussie made it to the top of the guardroom steps, where he collapsed. Old Bert Buchan smiled sadly and ordered up the meat wagon.

Aussie spent three weeks in British Military Hospital Hannover. 'Bloody great!' he informed me on discharge. 'Nip of rum and an injection.' He was in his usual position that night, perched on a stool in the corner of the NAAFI bar.

The orderly officer, a tall languid youth known to the Jocks as 'Hen Broon', stuck his head round the door just before closing.

'Hen, Hen!' roared Aussie.

'Yes, Potter,' said Hen, approaching warily.

'Been in hospital,' he was informed.

'The whole of the British Army of the Rhine knows you've been in hospital,' rejoined Hen.

'Yes, Sir, cured me of the rum for life, Sir; on the whisky now, Sir.'

Iain Mortimer

36. Envoi

It is alleged that in 1915 a Territorial Army Gordons battalion was marching by night on its way up to the front in France. It got lost.

The Adjutant was leading the way, and looked at his map with the Commanding Officer. The Commanding Officer said, 'Bill, I think we are near the Y of Ypres.'

The adjutant replied, 'With respect, Sir, I think we are near the S of Ypres.'

Out of the gloomy night came an old soldier, who leant over both of them and said, 'Weel, Sir – I think we are near the B of bloodywell lost.'

Lt-Gen. Sir Peter Graham

You have reached the last helping of the Gallimaufry. Can you help us to replenish the pot? Contributions to Volume 2 will be welcomed by Major Leslie Hatt, at 11 Delius Drive, Tonbridge, Kent TN10 4DW.

Glossary

Awa	away
Bachle	awkward, an odd ball
Bleezing	completely drunk
Bonnet	head-dress
Ca	turn
Chantie	chamber-pot
Crooshied	crocheted
Div	do
Fa	who
File	sometimes
Fit	what
Gallimaufry	a hash of odds and ends
Glowering	looking frowningly
Hae	have
Hale	whole
Heid	head
Hipes	dummy rifles
Hoose	house
Hunnert	hundred
Leerie	lamp-lighter
Mines	my own
Oot	out
Rax	search
Rickle	pile
Sae	so
Siccan	such
Skirly	white pudding
Steer	stirring